First Facts

Expert Pet Care

CARING

for

Rabbits

by Tammy Gagne

Raintree is an imprint of Capstone Global Library Limited, a company incorporated in England and Wales having its registered office at 264 Banbury Road, Oxford, OX2 7DY – Registered company number: 6695582

www.raintree.co.uk
myorders@raintree.co.uk

Edited by Marissa Kirkman
Designed by Sarah Bennett
Original illustrations © Capstone Global Library Limited 2019
Picture research by Tracy Cummins
Production by Laura Manthe
Originated by Capstone Global Library Ltd
Printed and bound in India

ISBN 978 1 4747 6090 4
22 21 20 19 18
10 9 8 7 6 5 4 3 2 1

British Library Cataloguing in Publication Data
A full catalogue record for this book is available from the British Library.

Acknowledgements
We would like to thank the following for permission to reproduce photographs: Alamy: Rosanne Tackaberry, 16; Capstone Studio: Karon Dubke, 7, 13, 19; Getty Images: Rebecca Emery, 17; iStockphoto: bunnylovinggrl, 6, cnicbc, 12, kali9, 15; Shutterstock: Africa Studio, 11 Bottom, Casey Williamson, 5, Dorottya Mathe, 21 Middle, Ear Iew Boo, 8, ekmelica, Design Element, Eric Isselee, 21 Bottom Left, IrinaK, 21 Bottom Right, JIANG HONGYAN, 3, Julia Kuznetsova, 9, kai_foret, 10, Linn Currie, 21 Top Right, Oleksandr Lytvynenko, Back Cover, 24, Olhastock, Cover, 23, Pentium5, 20, Santhosh Varghese, 11 Top, soportography, 18.

Every effort has been made to contact copyright holders of material reproduced in this book. Any omissions will be rectified in subsequent printings if notice is given to the publisher.

All the internet addresses (URLs) given in this book were valid at the time of going to press. However, due to the dynamic nature of the internet, some addresses may have changed, or sites may have changed or ceased to exist since publication. While the author and publisher regret any inconvenience this may cause readers, no responsibility for any such changes can be accepted by either the author or the publisher.

Contents

Your new pet rabbit

Rabbits are quiet, clever and playful pets. It is fun to watch them hop around. A rabbit may be the perfect pet for you. Make sure you are ready for the **responsibility** of owning a pet.

There are many different types of rabbits. Your family will need to choose which type of rabbit is right for you.

Look for a rabbit at an animal **shelter**. Many homeless animals can be found there.

responsibility duty or job

shelter place that takes care of, and rehomes lost or stray animals

4

Things you will need

You will need to buy some things for your rabbit, including a **hutch**. This is where your pet will sleep. Make sure the hutch is big enough for your pet to hop around. Your rabbit will also need bedding for its hutch, such as dust-free straw.

Your rabbit will need bowls for food and water. You can also use a water bottle for your pet. Make sure you buy chew toys for your rabbit too.

hutch cage used to house rabbits or other small pets

Bringing your rabbit home

Bringing your rabbit home is exciting. Many pet rabbits live in homes with cats and dogs. But be careful around other pets. A large dog could hurt a rabbit.

The best companion for a pet rabbit is another rabbit. Many owners say that it is easier to care for two rabbits than one. Rabbits are often more happy and friendly when kept together.

Guinea pigs and rabbits are sometimes kept together, but this is not the best companion for your rabbit.

What do rabbits eat?

Feed your rabbit hay each day. You can also give it a small amount of **pellets**. They contain many **vitamins** to help your pet stay healthy. Your rabbit will also need fresh water. Make sure you fill the bowl or bottle each day.

You can also feed small amounts of leafy green vegetables. Most rabbits eat parsley and spinach. Rabbits can be given small amounts of carrot as a treat.

FACT

Never give your rabbit corn, iceberg lettuce, potatoes or rhubarb. These foods can make your pet ill.

pellet small, hard piece of pet food

vitamin nutrient that helps keep people and animals healthy

This rabbit is eating pellets.

Keeping clean

Rabbits stay clean by licking themselves. But you must also brush your rabbit regularly. This helps your pet **shed** fur less often. It also keeps your rabbit from swallowing loose fur when cleaning itself.

Change your rabbit's straw bedding each day. You will also need to clean the hutch about once a week. Staying clean and dry will help keep your pet healthy.

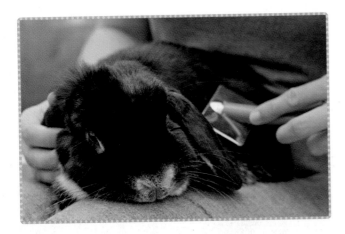

FACT

If you put a small tray at one end of the hutch, your pet may use it as a toilet. This will make cleaning the hutch a lot easier.

shed lose hair or fur

Going to the vet

Rabbits need to visit a **vet** just like other pets. Take your rabbit once a year for a check-up. You will also need to take your rabbit to a vet if it is injured or unwell.

You should have your rabbit **neutered**. This will stop your rabbit from having babies. It will also make your rabbit a calmer and healthier pet.

Male rabbits can be neutered at 12 weeks of age. Female rabbits can be neutered at 16 weeks.

vet doctor trained to take care of animals

neuter operate on an animal so it is unable to produce young

Life with a rabbit

Regular exercise keeps rabbits healthy. Make sure your rabbit has a chance to hop, run and jump each day.

Some people keep their rabbits indoors instead of outside. If you keep your rabbit indoors, you must make the room safe. Make sure, for example, that there are no electric cables that your rabbit could chew.

Indoor rabbits can play in toy tunnels.

Your rabbit may prefer to be outside. Ask your vet or staff at the shelter about keeping your rabbit indoors to make sure this is the right thing for your particular pet.

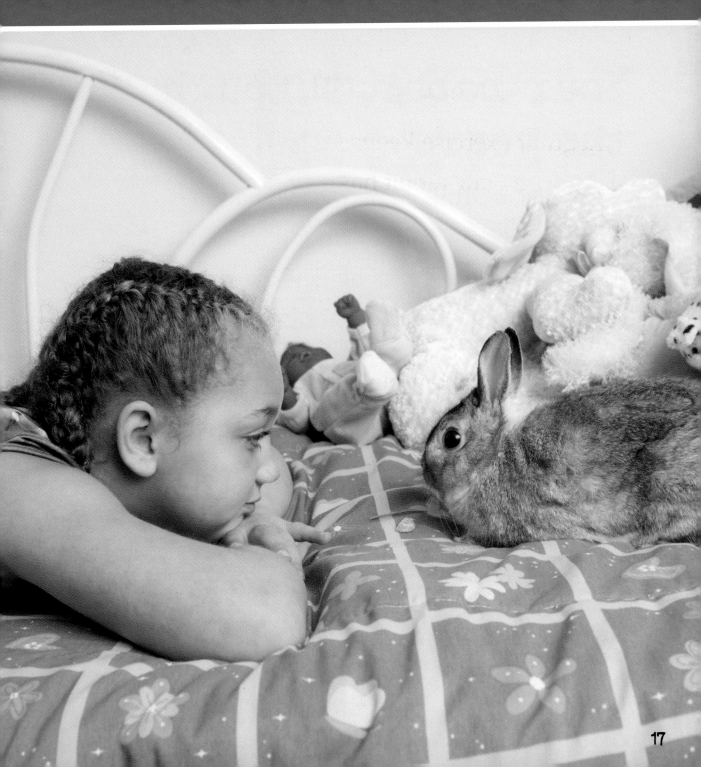

Your rabbit through the years

Rabbits are full of energy. Even adult rabbits spend a lot of time hopping and playing. But as your rabbit gets older, some changes will take place.

Rabbits who are five years or older are called **senior** pets. Your older rabbit will rest more and play less than it did before. Senior rabbits can become overweight if owners are not careful. You may need to cut back on the amount of pellets you feed your senior pet.

senior older than someone else; a senior pet is an older animal

When well cared for, rabbits can live for 8 to 12 years.

Rabbit body language

You can watch your rabbit's **behaviour** to see how it is feeling. An excited rabbit will run and jump in a dancing motion. This move is called a binky. A rabbit that feels safe will quickly roll onto its side. This is called a flop.

An angry rabbit will sometimes growl. It is important to leave your rabbit alone if it makes this sound.

behaviour way a person or an animal behaves

Types of rabbits

Long-haired rabbits:

- Angora rabbits
- Jersey woolly rabbits
- Lionhead rabbits.

Jersey wooly rabbit

Lionhead rabbit

Short-haired rabbits:

- American rabbits
- Belgian hares
- Dutch rabbits.

Belgian hare

Dutch rabbit

Glossary

behaviour way a person or an animal behaves

hutch cage used to house rabbits or other small pets

neuter operate on an animal so it is unable to produce young

pellet small, hard piece of pet food

responsibility duty or job

senior older than someone else; a senior pet is an older animal

shed lose hair or fur

shelter place that takes care of, and rehomes, lost or stray animals

vet doctor trained to take care of animals

vitamin nutrient that helps keep people and animals healthy

Find out more

Books

All About Rabbits and Other Small Animals (RSPCA), Anita Ganeri (Scholastic, 2013)

Bunny's Guide to Caring for Your Rabbit (Pets' Guides), Anita Ganeri (Raintree, 2014)

Looking After Rabbits (Pet Guides), Fiona Patchett (Usborne, 2013)

Rabbits (Animal Family Albums), Charlotte Guillain (Raintree, 2014)

The Truth About Rabbits: What Rabbits Do When You're Not Looking (Pets Undercover!), Mary Colson (Raintree, 2018)

Websites

Find out more about pet care at:
www.dkfindout.com/uk/animals-and-nature/pet-care

Learn more about all sorts of animals and how to take care of them at:
young.rspca.org.uk/kids/animals

Comprehension questions

1. When is it safe for your rabbit to be neutered?
2. What foods are dangerous for your pet rabbit?
3. How can you tell if your rabbit is excited?

Index